Life in the Middle Ages

Story by **Evelyne Brisou-Pellen**
Factual accounts by **Antoine Sabbagh**
Activities by **Béatrice Garel**
Game by **Catherine Pauwels**

BARRON'S

contents

Story

William's Return   4

Mega-infos

Medieval People:
   Much Like Us   12
Most People Were Peasants   14
The Castle Stronghold   16
Religion at the Center of
   Everyday Life   18
In the Heart of the Forests   20
Town Life   22

Activity

Making a Seal   24

Mega-infos

Pilgrims and Travelers   26
Masters and Apprentices   28
Meals and Feasts   30

Activity

Prepare a Medieval Meal   32

Mega-infos

The Great Plagues   34
Strangers and Outcasts   36

Anecdotes

Incredible but True!   38

Mega-infos

The Position of Women   40

Hygiene and Beauty   42

Fashions and Costumes   44

Festivals and Carnivals   46

Game

A Palace Ball   48

Mega-infos

Churches and Cathedrals   50

The King and the Lords   52

The Art of Warfare   54

Masterpieces of the
   Middle Ages   56

Quiz

True or False?   58

Index   62

62

Answers   63

63

Stickers

Picture Cards

William's Return

Evelyne Brisou-Pellen

The Return of the Son

"Dame Yolande," cried Doda, "I can see dust rising on the road. A horseman is coming! . . . No, two horsemen!"

"Good heavens, do you think it is William already?"

"I think so," replied the servant. "The messenger who told us of his return said he was two days distant, but your son must have been in such a hurry that a single day was enough."

"Good heavens," Dame Yolande repeated. "My son! It's ten years since I've seen him, ten years since he left for the Crusades, ten years that he has been a prisoner of the Turks! . . . Quickly, lower the drawbridge!"

There was a loud noise of hooves, then two horses entered the castle courtyard. A handsome knight jumped to the ground and took Dame Yolande into his arms.

"Mother, how good it is to see you again!"

"You have returned at last, my son!" Dame Yolande cried as she hugged him. "I hardly recognized you!"

"You shouldn't be so surprised," said William, "I was only fifteen when I left. But you, Mother, haven't changed at all. And here is Master Albaldus. What good fortune! Do you remember how cross I made you when I refused to learn how to shoot a bow?"

"The only weapon that you liked," responded Albaldus, "was . . ."

". . . Was the sword. I fear that I was a difficult pupil. But here is Doda, my dear nurse! How pleased I am that you are still here. I hope that you have forgiven all the naughty tricks that I played on you!"

"I have forgotten them all," said Doda, laughing, "because I am so happy to see you again."

"Have you even forgotten the day when I tore up all the tablecloths to make ropes?"

Doda laughed again.

"Go and clean up at the fountain, my son," suggested Dame Yolande, "while I give orders to prepare a feast. We shall celebrate your return!"

William strode towards the fountain, followed by his servant, who whispered to his master.

"It's working! They think you are William. It's true that with your beard, you do look like him."

"It's been a long time since these people have seen him, and between fifteen and twenty-five a person changes a lot."

"All the same, take care. I have the impression that they are suspicious, and that the old man may have been testing you when he spoke of the only arms that you liked."

"I brought it off well, though, didn't I? It was not too hard. When William and I were prisoners together, we had plenty of time to talk. He described his family so well that I recognized them all. But don't worry, I'll be careful."

"What are we going to do now?"

"Don't worry about a thing. We're here, and God knows where William is. What we must do is take charge of the castle's affairs. Then we'll be rich. Rich!"

Curiosity and Doubts

Dame Yolande was thoughtful. Certainly, her son had suffered for ten years in filthy prisons. No doubt that was why he had changed so much. Besides, how could he not be William? He knew them all and remembered everything from his earlier life. Or did he?

When they were sitting down to dinner she said, amiably, "Well, my son, you seem to like this cod pie."

"Yes indeed, it is delicious."

"Ah, you used to hate it!"

William looked squarely at Dame Yolande and burst out laughing.

"That's because I've had a taste of prison food and have become less spoiled. When my stomach was tortured with hunger, I would have given my right hand for a slice of this pie."

Everyone started to laugh, and Dame Yolande was reassured. He may have been a picky eater as a child, but he had always had an appetite!

Then William said "Rest assured, mother, my father's murder by the cursed Turks has been avenged. I have killed dozens of them with my own hands."

Dame Yolande only said "Thank you, my son." Then she excused herself, blaming a headache. She went to her room, where her servant was waiting.

"Well, Doda, what do you say to that?"

"I don't know, Madame. It's true that after the death of your husband, we decided never to admit that he was

burned at the stake for sorcery. We told everyone that he was killed by the Turks."

"But my son knew that was not true."

"After all this time, perhaps your son has persuaded himself that his father really was a hero."

"Could you truly think so? In any case, he had no need to speak of it and stir up old wounds. Yes, it seems strange that my son should do such a thing."

Dame Yolande looked out of the window and thought.

He who Thought Himself the Deceiver Was Himself Deceived

The next day Dame Yolande made an announcement. "My son, I have a surprise for you. Your foster sister, Millicent, has hurried over as soon as she heard of your return. Here she is now."

The imposter hesitated for a moment. The Devil! He couldn't remember the real William talking about a foster sister! Last night he had noticed Dame Yolande react with the slightest look of surprise when he recalled the death of "his" father. Had the real William not told him the whole truth? He must not make any more mistakes!

"Millicent!" he cried happily, "I would not have recognized you! What a beautiful woman you have become!"

"Come now, was I not just as pretty when we were children?" retorted Millicent laughingly.

"Of course, you have always been pretty," William replied, "but I was too young to appreciate it."

Dame Yolande departed without a word and retired to her room. William had never had a foster sister. She had invented Millicent herself and asked one of the servants to play the role. This man was not William! But what to do? She was a widow of a minor lord. Her men were loyal, but they were few. She hated the thought that these rogues might fight and injure some of them. And she *must* find out about William!

She went down on her knees and prayed. No sooner had she said "Amen" when a plan was born, fully formed, in her mind. She called for Doda.

Doda approached "William's" servant and looked suspiciously to right and left before whispering "Hey! You! It's all up. You've been found out! Tonight, your master will be captured by the guards. He'll be put to the torture until he confesses to William's murder. Tomorrow morning at dawn he will be beheaded. You will be sold as a slave!"

The servant turned white. "Why are you telling me this?

"You remind me of my brother who died 24 years ago. In spite of your sins, I wish no harm to come to you. I will even tell you of a way out of the castle without being seen. But first you must tell me, is William alive?"

"I don't know. When we were released, we traveled together. Then we were set upon by bandits. William fought and we fled. We thought we saw him fall."

"My God," cried Doda. "Then what happened?"

"We did not see William again. But we began thinking. He was returning to a family, an estate, while we had nothing. Therefore, as my brother resembles him a little, we decided to pretend he was William."

Doda was furious. "You are rogues and cowards. But I am not your judge. Pray that God forgives you! Now here is the way out. Go to the end of this hall . . ."

It was the black of night. Dame Yolande and Doda stood at the window. Suddenly, there was a great splash, then another.

"Good," said Doda. "They have opened the lower door and fallen into the moat."

"In a few moments," said Dame Yolande, "they will climb out, frightened by their fall and numb with cold. They will dash away as fast as they can."

The two women stared out the window into the darkness. Suddenly they saw a bright point of light. Someone was out

riding with a torch. A memory tugged at
her. William had said something to her
before he had left so many years ago. "If
I return at night I shall light first one torch,
then another, so you shall know that it is
me." Dame Yolande's heart beat strongly
in her breast as the light came closer. Then
a second point of light joined the first.

Her spirits soared. Her prayers answered,
she awaited the arrival of her true son.

Medieval People

The medieval period (or Middle Ages) lasted about 1,000 years—roughly from 500 A.D. until 1500 A.D. During these centuries, everyday life changed very little.

Were They Different from Us?

Well-preserved human bodies, over 1,000 years old, have been found in swamps. They show that people back then were very much like us, though they were often shorter. This can be explained by the poor quality of their diet. But there were also some very tall people, just as there are today.

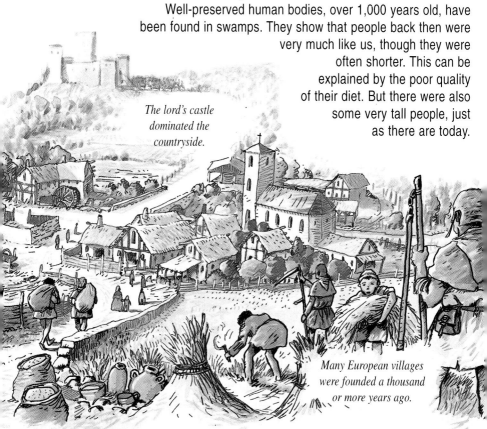

The lord's castle dominated the countryside.

Many European villages were founded a thousand or more years ago.

ʌuch Like Us

Hardier People

Because they spent most of their time in the open air, people became very tough. Only the well-to-do had horses; the rest traveled everywhere on foot. Rich and poor alike lived in poorly heated houses, and the climate was colder than it is today. There were so few doctors and so little medicine, that people learned to live with their pains and injuries.

A Shorter Lifespan

Death at an early age was common. Disease, famines, and wars kept the population low. Many children died just after birth. Few people lived longer than 50 years. At the age of 13, boys and girls were considered adults. Young teenagers went out to work and war, married, and had children.

A Reassuring Landscape

Many European villages were founded over a thousand years ago. Some areas, however, remained deserted. Seashores with their wild waves, deep forests, and mountains were feared for their danger and mystery. People preferred to live in the flat countryside, crowded close together in villages.

Time Stood Still

There were no clocks. Days passed to the rhythm of church bells and farm work. Events were repeated from season to season and year to year. People lived as their parents and grandparents had. Progress was very, very slow.

Most People Were Peasant:

Throughout Europe, the vast majority of people were peasant farmers.

■ Houses

A typical house was a single room, with a fire for both heating and cooking. The floor was of packed earth, the walls of dried mud, the roof of thatched straw. Windows, if any, were tiny and unglazed. Furniture was scarce. A peasant family was lucky if it had a rough table and a few stools. Storage chests and beds were prized possessions. Often the whole family would sleep in one bed!

■ Tools and Progress

Most peasants worked with wooden tools edged with metal. Because they were so poorly equipped, medieval farmers had very poor crops. For each grain of wheat sown, only three were reaped—a small fraction of yields today. During the twelfth century new plows with iron blades came into use. The introduction of the shoulder collar allowed draft animals to pull twice as much as before. Peasants began clearing the forests and working new lands.

City-dwellers ("citizens") had no land. They purchased food from peasants who brought it from the countryside.

■ The Calendar

For the peasants, each season had its tasks. In autumn, they sowed wheat. In winter, they butchered their pigs and repaired their tools. In spring, they planted oats. At harvest time, they worked together to bring in the crops. They helped each other whenever someone's fields were lying *fallow*❦. Mostly they grew cereals, with a few vegetables and perhaps some livestock.

❦*Fallow:*
Medieval farmers would let a field rest every two or three years. This allowed the soil to recover some of its fertility.

■ Freemen and Serfs

Free peasants were few and far between. They paid the lord a *tax*❦ for the right to farm a piece of his land. They also had to pay fees to use his mill and oven. Lowest of all were the serfs who worked in the lord's fields. Considered his property, they were not allowed to leave the land.

❦*Tax, or rent, was paid in labor (performed in the lord's fields) or with a portion of the freeman's crop.*

The Castle Stronghold

The castle was the lord's residence. Often attacked, it also sheltered the peasants in times of danger.

■ Castle Construction

The castle was headquarters and home to a military leader. Early versions were often made of wood, raised up on a mound of earth. From the tenth century onward, castles developed into mighty stone fortresses. Built on high ground from which danger could be seen at a distance, the castle had strong walls, sometimes 12 feet (4 meters) thick at the base. Within the walls, was a courtyard dominated by a sturdy tower called the *keep.*

■ The Protection of Powerful Lords

The great emperor Charlemagne ruled much of Western Europe. But his empire fell apart after his death in 814 A.D. Local warlords acted like kings, forcing their will on their subjects. But in times of danger, the serfs could take refuge in the castles.

❦ Hunting

A favorite sport of the nobility, hunting was forbidden to the peasants. (See page 20 for further discussion.)

■ Castle Life

Living like a lord meant not having to work. Noble lords passed their time riding horses, fighting, and *hunting.*❦ Each lord had his own court, at which he entertained friends. The nobles would feast while watching jugglers and listening to stories that were sung and told by minstrels.

■ The Siege

An enemy troop approaches. Lookouts sound the alarm. The drawbridge is raised. Archers take their positions. Others prepare boiling water, oil, or molten lead, to pour on the enemy. The enemy soldiers smash at the gate with a battering ram and try to scale the walls. They have even brought up a massive wooden siege tower on rollers made from logs. All is in vain, however. This time the fortress will stand firm.

Religion at the Cente

Missionaries from Rome, Ireland, and Constantinople converted all of Europe to Christianity.

■ At the Heart of the Village: The Church

At the center of every town was the church. People gathered there for Sunday Mass. For every problem they went to see the priest. He comforted the ill and prayed for the souls of the people. The church was a sacred place. People went there for protection from attack. Armed men were forbidden to enter.

)f Everyday Life

Rites for Every Occasion

Religion was a vital part of every moment of a person's life. When a child was born, it was brought to the church to be baptized. When a person was dying, someone ran to find the priest to say the final prayer. Before each meal, the father traced a cross on the crust of the bread. Many people tried to pray all day long. At work, people listened for the sound of church bells announcing the hours and calling them to prayer.

Monks and Monasteries

Religious communities, or *monasteries,* multiplied from the seventh century onwards. The greatest number belonged to the Benedictine Order, founded in Italy by Saint Benedict in 540 A.D. Monks prayed, copied manuscripts, and worked. Monasteries received many donations, and some grew very wealthy. They became centers of culture, but also places of refuge and safety for travelers and the very poor.

Beliefs

Every event in life—a good harvest or a drought, a birth or a death, a plague or a war—was explained as the Will of God. God, the supreme and all-powerful being, either punished people or rewarded them. When they died, the good went to Heaven and the wicked went to Hell. People would ask priests and monks to offer prayers on their behalf. They also went to the tombs of the saints. There, they would touch relics, hoping that the sacred bones or clothes could produce miracles.

In the Heart of the Forests

In the Middle Ages, the forest was actually more important than the cultivated land. Even though it could be frightening, the forest was the center of the peasant economy. It also provided a rich game preserve for the lords.

Mega-infos

◼ The Forest: A Source of Raw Materials

Most everyday tools and objects (spoons, plates, stools) were made from wood. Wood was used in the construction of houses, carts, and boats. In some areas, it was the only fuel available for heating and cooking. It also supplied the charcoal needed to make glass and work metal.

◼ The Forest: An Essential Food Reserve

All kinds of foods were found in the forests: wild fruit, nuts, and mushrooms. Acorns were gathered and ground into flour. People let their animals forage for food in the forest. Wild game was plentiful. Nobles reserved for themselves the right to hunt large animals such as deer, leaving only small game like squirrels and rabbits for the peasants to snare.

◼ The Forest as a Place of Refuge

In the forest you might meet solitary hermits, bears and wolves, bandits, and serfs who had run away from their lords. Sometimes these outcasts lived together in small camps. The English tale of Robin Hood describes such a band of outlaws living in Sherwood Forest near Nottingham.

◼ The Enchanted World of the Forests

The forests were full of strange noises and eerie silences—definitely not the sort of places to go strolling for fun. You could get lost there! It was supposed that fabulous beings might dwell in them. Perhaps you would encounter fairies, witches, and trolls, or you might happen upon a unicorn, or even a dragon!

Town Life

Wealthy and few in number, the towns had to struggle for their freedom and independence.

▨ The Towns: Protected Places

Protected by a ring of powerful walls, called *ramparts,* towns of the Middle Ages were often small in size. Inside the walls were wooden houses packed tightly together, churches and perhaps stone palaces, but also gardens. Some towns even grew fields of grain within their walls. Walled towns had gates that were closed for the night.

▨ Towns as Centers of Wealth

Towns were places of trade. Peasants brought their produce to sell, or exchange for manufactured items such as fabric, furniture, and tools. Money changers could also be found—they were the bankers of the Middle Ages. The best known of these commercial towns sponsored regular trade fairs to which people came from far and wide.

▨ Always Under Threat

In times of war, the inhabitants of besieged towns risked starvation. The inhabitants were also faced with other dangers. Almost everything was built of wood. In case of fire, all water had to be drawn from wells and streams by hand—making firefighting difficult or impossible. The lack of sanitation—there were no sewers—made towns into breeding grounds for vermin and diseases.

■ The Towns Gain Their Independence

From the beginning of the tenth century, some wealthy towns began to acquire their independence, often by fighting against the king or the lords. These free towns were run by the leading *bourgeois*🍎 families. Many such centers of trade and manufacturing developed in Belgium, the northern parts of France, Germany, and Italy.

> 🍎*Bourgeois: a term used to describe the new "middle class" of merchants and other wealthy townspeople.*

■ Great Cities of the Middle Ages

With 200,000 inhabitants in the thirteenth century, Paris was the largest city in Europe, followed by Venice. Next came London, followed by Bruges in Belgium, and the German cities of Hanover and Lübeck.

Makin

All important people possessed a seal—a piece of metal or stone engraved with their personal emblem. The seal was pressed into a lump of melted sealing wax. Seals were usually considered more reliable than signatures. The king's seal on an order, or that of a merchant on a load of merchandise, were guarantees of authenticity.

You will need:
- a cork from a bottle
- a button with a raised design, or a coin
- glue
- some wax from a candle

1. Put some glue on the cork.

2. Glue the button onto the cork. Wait for it to dry.

Seal

4. Push your seal into the center of the wax.

3. Knead a ball of wax with your fingers until it is soft. Put it on your document and squash it with your thumb.

Pilgrims and Travelers

In the Middle Ages, traveling was a dangerous adventure. Roads were unsafe because of bandits and thieves. There was also the risk of getting lost. The longest journey most people made was a pilgrimage to a local saint's tomb.

■ Journeys in the Middle Ages

Usually, people traveled on foot. Only the wealthy rode on horseback. Journeys lasted for weeks, months, or even years. The slowest travel was by water.

■ The Great Pilgrimage Routes

The most frequently used routes led to major pilgrimage sites—to Rome where the Pope lived, Santiago de Compostella in Spain where St. James was buried, and Jerusalem in the Holy Land. People went on pilgrimages to pray for forgiveness of their sins and for healing of their illnesses.

The Great Stages

On the road it was wise to be wary of isolated inns, which could be hideouts for bandits. It was better to seek sanctuary in a monastery or a town. Journeys were planned in stages, first to one place, then to the next, and so on, until the final destination was reached. If you were a noble, you could also request shelter at the castles of other nobles.

Men of the Road and Wanderers

Most people, the peasants, went no farther than the local market. Travelers were nicknamed "dusty feet" because they became covered with dirt from the unpaved roads. Many were pilgrims, but you could also meet merchants, soldiers, students and, more worryingly, beggars, or even bandits ready to confront you with the cry, "Your money or your life!"

Noble women usually traveled in wagons.

Masters and

During the thirteenth century, textiles developed into the largest industry in Europe.

The windmill and the horizontal loom were both invented during the Middle Ages.

An Industrial Revolution in the Middle Ages

After centuries of poverty and backwardness, new inventions began to make life easier. Wind and water mills were built to supply the energy to grind grain, cut wood, and manufacture new materials such as paper. Mines were opened, providing silver for commerce and iron for tools and weapons. The economy improved.

Masters and Craftsmen

In the twelfth century, textile manufacturing grew rapidly. Many peasants left their farms to seek work in the towns. Exceptionally skillful workers became apprentices who learned the craft of weaving wool, linen, and sometimes silk. Eventually, the best workers might become craftsmen and set up shops of their own.

The great merchants bought and sold textiles all over Europe.

Apprentices

■ Rich Merchants

The shops depended on the orders of the rich cloth merchants, or drapers, who bought up the cloth and resold it. The rich nobles of the time loved to dress up. Sometimes the king might order thousands of blankets for the army. In Flanders (part of modern Belgium) and Italy, the drapers became so rich and powerful that they actually ran their towns!

■ The Misery of the Textile Workers

"We will always be poor and naked, always hungry and thirsty." Thus spoke the miserable weavers described by *Christian of Troyes.*✿ Workers were paid very little and were treated so harshly that they sometimes led armed revolts against the merchants who controlled their lives. In spite of the terrible conditions, serfs continued to flee to the towns.

> ✿*Christian of Troyes, 1135–1183, was one of the earliest poets who wrote in the language that became modern French.*

■ The Luxury Crafts

The most skillful craftsmen made luxury goods for the nobility and the church. Furriers, cabinet-makers, master carvers, glassblowers, and goldsmiths all thrived in great cities like Paris, Cologne, and Florence.

Meals and Feasts

In the Middle Ages, there was always the threat of famine. On festival days, however, meals could become glorious feasts.

Salmon, meat pie, leg of venison, and mutton might all be served at banquets.

The Poor Man's Table

Dark bread made of rye flour, soup, a few vegetables, an egg every now and then—this was the diet of the poor. On festival days, there might be some pork in their wooden bowls. (Because pigs would eat almost anything, they were the most commonly raised animal.)

The Rich Man's Table

The meals of the lords and the rich town dwellers included plenty of meat, eaten on plates of precious metal. There was no refrigeration, however, so old meat would be heavily spiced to cover up the smell. Everyone ate with their hands. Spoons and forks did not come into use until later.

The Threat of Famine

Composed almost entirely of grains, the diet of the poor in the Middle Ages was not well balanced, but it did allow them to live and work. However, bad weather or a poor harvest were common catastrophes. Then, both the towns and the countryside suffered from famine and disease.

ginger

nutmeg

cardamom

cinnamon

Brought back from the Orient by the Crusaders, spices became widespread.

What Did They Drink?

Water usually came from a nearby river, which was also used for laundry, bathing, and watering animals. In the towns, tanneries and dye works polluted the streams. Clean wells and natural springs were jealously guarded. For lack of good water most people, even children, drank beer, cider, and wine.

Prepare a Medieval Meal

In the Middle Ages, a thick slice of bread, called a trencher, often served as a plate. At the end of the meal, the "plate" itself was eaten!

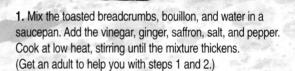

■ Green Eggs and Cheese
(for 4 people)

Ingredients:
- 8 eggs
- 4 slices of toast or stale bread (trenchers)
- 3 slices of crumbled toast
- 1 bouillon cube
- 1 pinch of sugar
- 1 pinch of saffron
- 1 tablespoon of vinegar
- 2½ ounces (70 grams) grated Swiss cheese
- 1 tablespoon chopped parsley
- salt and pepper to taste
- ¾ cup of water

1. Mix the toasted breadcrumbs, bouillon, and water in a saucepan. Add the vinegar, ginger, saffron, salt, and pepper. Cook at low heat, stirring until the mixture thickens. (Get an adult to help you with steps 1 and 2.)

2. Bring 1½ quarts (1.5 liters) of water to a simmer in a saucepan. Poach the eggs by breaking them gently, one by one, into the water. Carefully mix the whites and yolks together with a large spoon. Let each egg cook for 2 minutes.

3. Lift the eggs out of the saucepan with a slotted spoon and put them on the trenchers.

4. Add the chopped parsley and cheese to the sauce, stir, and pour over the eggs.

Activity

Fruit Turnovers
(for 4 people)

Ingredients:
- 7¹/₄ ounces (210 grams) of pastry dough
- 3 apples, peeled and cored
- 3¹/₂ ounces (100 grams) of figs
- 3¹/₂ ounces (100 grams) of raisins
- 2¹/₂ ounces (70 grams) of shelled nuts
- 2 tablespoons honey
- 1 teaspoon cinnamon

1. Soak the raisins in water until they are plump and tender.

2. Chop the apples, figs, and nuts into small pieces. Dry the raisins on a towel, then mix everything together.

3. Add the honey and spices. Mix thoroughly.

4. Cut out circles of pastry dough using a large glass or a jar. Put some of the mixture in the middle of each circle.

5. Dampen the edges of the pastry dough and shape into turnovers. Seal the edges with the prongs of a fork.

6. Ask an adult to help you bake the turnovers in the oven at 325 degrees Fahrenheit (175 degrees Celsius) for 30 minutes.

Almond Milk
(for 4 people)

Ingredients:
- 1 slice of bread, toasted and crumbled
- 3¹/₂ ounces (100 grams) of almond powder
- 1 tablespoon orange blossom water
- 1 quart (about 1 liter) of milk
- 2 tablespoons of honey

1. Put all the ingredients into a saucepan. Ask an adult to help you simmer the mixture for 5 minutes, stirring constantly.

2. Mix for a few seconds in a blender or mixer, then pour through a fine strainer.

3. Serve warm.

The Great Plagues

Time after time, terrible epidemics, called plagues, raged through Europe.

■ Poor Nutrition and Lots of Dirt

Bad food, poor housing, famine, and war weakened people. They fell ill more often than we do today, and their illnesses were often worse. Many people died of diseases at an early age.

▪ Illness in the Middle Ages

Paintings from the Middle Ages show beggars with sunken eyes and wasted faces. Epidemics of influenza and the measles also ravaged the population. Miserable lepers, with their horrible sores, were banished from towns and had to live apart. People had no idea of how diseases spread. Many thought the epidemics were punishment sent by God.

▪ The Black Death

In 1348, merchants from the Italian city of Genoa returned home from Asia. They brought back a terrible new illness with them. Transmitted by fleas from rats, the "Black Death" spread like wildfire throughout Europe. It is estimated that a quarter of the population of Europe died during the first few years of the plague.

▪ The Secrets of Medicine

There were no schools for doctors. In the countryside, bonesetters and herb gatherers (who were sometimes accused of sorcery) repaired fractures and made healing potions. In towns some barbers practiced a bit of surgery and bloodletting—the favorite treatment for almost everything. No one knew anything about diseases, and Church doctrine forbade the exploration of the inside of the body.

Strangers and Outcasts

People were afraid of strangers and outcasts, whom they frequently blamed for any misfortune that might befall them.

◼ The Fear of Strangers

Most people knew only their own neighbors and were suspicious of all strangers. Whoever was not from the village was an outsider—and probably up to no good. Travelers would always attract suspicion. Why weren't they home working? Whenever anything bad happened, the stranger was always to blame.

◼ Beggars and Lepers

Afflicted with a terrible skin disease, lepers were not allowed close to the villages. They signaled their approach by ringing a bell. Beggars were everywhere, creating awful spectacles in the town squares. And organized bands of muggers and thieves were regularly broken up by men-at-arms.

◼ The Jews—a Segregated Community

Few in number, Jews in medieval Europe were forbidden to farm or own land. Restricted to certain areas (called *ghettos*), they often worked directly for the king. Their persecution began at about the same time as the Crusades. Forced to wear a distinctive sign on their clothes, they were often expelled and sometimes were massacred.

▪ Muslims and Christians

In the early Middle Ages, Muslims ruled in Spain and southern Italy. They tolerated Christians when they were in power. But when the Christians started their *Crusades*❦ to seize the Holy Land, the Muslims were portrayed as monsters in league with the Devil. After Christians reconquered Spain, the Muslims were expelled.

❦*Crusade: One of the several Christian expeditions to capture the sacred places in Palestine.*

Incredible

○ A KING WHO PERFORMED MIRACLES

In France, the king was a sacred person, the representative of God on Earth. People were convinced that he could perform miracles. After the coronation of the French king in the cathedral at Reims, people suffering from *scrofula*, a skin disease, came before him. The king touched the ill people and doctors then declared that all traces of the disease had disappeared. "The king touched you . . . . The king healed you," they would say.

● ANIMALS USED TO MAKE WAR

Towards the end of the Middle Ages, English archers used powerful longbows made of wood from yew trees. On the eve of the Battle of Agincourt, a decisive battle of the Hundred Years War, the French released hungry rats in the English camp. They hoped the starving animals would gnaw away at the bow strings, which were made of pig gut. But the English had brought along cats, and their bows were saved. Each army also had large, savage war-dogs. To make them harder to catch, the dogs' ears and tails were cropped.

ut True!

RELICS

In the Middle Ages, monasteries and churches attracted more pilgrims if they had precious relics of saints. Nobody doubted that the old clothes and bones were genuine. For example, St. Riquier, in the north of France, had a scrap of Christ's robe, a piece of bread from the Last Supper, hairs from St. Paul's beard, the original stones that had been used to kill St. Stephen (still covered with his blood), and even some milk from the Virgin Mary!

CONVERTING THE UNBELIEVERS

In order to convert the pagan Saxons, Charlemagne did not hesitate to burn down their villages. Once, in a single day, he killed 5,000 people who refused to accept Christ as the saviour. Four centuries earlier, St. Colomban had used a novel way to convert the Irish, who had murdered the missionaries sent before him. When he arrived in their villages, he knelt down, formed a cross with his arms, and stayed as still as a statue for hours, days, and weeks on end. The Irish people were so fascinated that they ended up joining him.

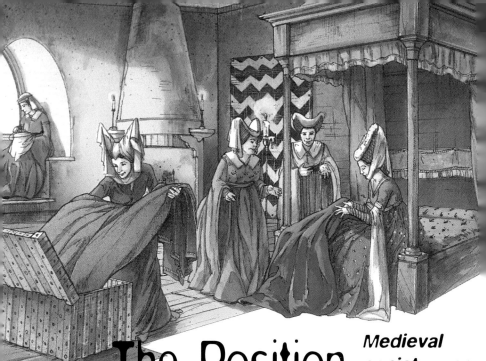

The Position of Women

Medieval society was dominated by men, but women played an essential role, both at home and at work.

■ Women Worked Everywhere

Peasant women tended the house, raised the children, and did the cooking. They also collected firewood, looked after the farmyard, and bled the pigs when they were slaughtered. Sometimes they pulled the plows along with the men. In the towns women also worked at spinning and weaving. Even when they were pregnant, women continued working. They stopped only briefly to give birth.

Mega-infos

■ The Ladies' Room

In the lords' houses the women's quarters formed a world apart. The lord's wife looked after the upkeep of the house and brought up the children—boys until the age of six, and girls until they were grown. Rooms in the castle were set aside for her and her attendant ladies.

■ Courtly Love

Warriors, whose lives had been brutal and violent for centuries, began to adopt a new attitude towards women. A knight would attend his lady at court and wear her colors into battle. Courtesy toward women became as important as courage under attack. Brave, chivalrous gentlemen were the heroes of courtly love stories, such as the *Tales of King Arthur*.

Isabella of Spain

■ Great Heroines of the Middle Ages

In the Middle Ages the most revered woman was the Virgin Mary, the mother of Christ. From the twelfth century on more churches were dedicated to her than to anyone else. Examples of real-life heroines were strong and ruthless queens, like Eleanor of Aquitaine and Isabella of Spain, and of course the heroic war leader Joan of Arc.

Joan of Arc played a major role during the Hundred Years War.

Hygiene and Beauty

Cleanliness was not a matter of concern in the Middle Ages. People washed very little. Public baths did exist in some large cities, but they were used mostly for pleasure.

Neither Water nor Toilets

In ancient Rome, each wealthy household had a bath. There was even some running water and indoor plumbing in that city. These luxuries did not exist in the Middle Ages. Even the rich got their water from wells or rivers. Instead of toilets, everyone used chamber pots or outdoor privies, which were little more than holes in the ground.

The War Against Lice

In the Middle Ages people were always scratching themselves because they were covered with fleas and lice. It was considered uncultured to scratch in public. At home, however, it was quite normal to pick lice from your hair and clothes.

Elementary Hygiene

Washing the hands and face were the only acts of everyday hygiene. People rarely changed their clothes. Queen Isabella of Spain swore that she would not change her shirt until the city of Grenada was liberated from Muslim hands. That happened in 1492. Her shirt became black, giving rise to a noble synonym for that color: *sable*.

The Pleasures of the Bath

In the early Middle Ages, many towns and villages had steam baths and bathing pools. People went more to socialize in the water than to get clean. The Church, however, was wary of men and women bathing together. Little by little, these baths were closed.

Beauty Secrets

In the Middle Ages, smelling nice and having good breath were luxuries that only refined people could hope to achieve. Rich women coated their skin with perfumed oint-ments and oils. They chewed cinnamon, licorice, fennel, and other herbs.

Fashions and Costumes

Above all else, clothes needed to be practical and warm. Among the nobility, the fashion was for colorful clothes made of rich, showy materials.

■ Everyday Clothes

"The habit does not make the monk," says a medieval proverb. However, it was by their costumes that people were recognized. Peasants wore rough, homemade clothes. These would be kept as long as possible and patched over and over again. Monks and nuns had their distinctive habits. Wealthy merchants and nobles wore brightly colored outfits of fine wool and precious silk.

Noblemen and merchants could be distinguished by their clothes: fur for the noblemen, long robes for the merchants.

■ Pointed Hats and Pointed Shoes

At the end of the Middle Ages, the nobility wore elaborate, tight-fitting clothes. Women liked to keep their hair covered in public, and the fashion was for tall, cone-shaped steeple-hats. Men wore shoes with long, pointed toes that curled upward.

◼ Fur

At the end of the Middle Ages the climate was extremely cold. For protection, nothing could match fur coats turned fur side in. Those who could afford it used rabbit or fox skins, and also the much sought-after otter and sable. Ermine was the most valuable fur, so rare it was reserved for royalty.

◼ Fashionable Colors

The poor wore drab, undyed fabrics. Rich people wore colorful clothes. Little by little, blue became the fashionable color with knights, and red for gentlewomen. Stripes were sometimes associated with the Devil! Monks and nuns dressed in black, brown, or white, symbols of humility, poverty, and purity.

Festivals and Carnivals

Church holidays provided opportunities for games and merrymaking.

Religious Festivals

There were no vacations in the Middle Ages, but there were many religious festivals—at least 100 each year. The most important ones were Christmas and Easter. Next came St. John's Day in June, which marked the beginning of summer, and the Feast of the Virgin in August.

◼ An Occasion for Theater

Holy days were not all prayers and solemnity. In front of the cathedral was a circus of jugglers, acrobats, dancing bears, and other spectacles. Then, there might be a slapstick comedy—such as the traditional puppet show, *Punch and Judy.* Finally, costumed actors standing on a platform would present scenes from the life of a saint.

◼ All the Fun of the Carnival

The Church decreed 40 days of prayer and fasting before Easter, called *Lent.* During this time the eating of meat was forbidden. The last day before the beginning of the fast was a riotous holiday. In Italy the people cried "Carne vale!," meaning *the meat is leaving.*

◼ Hullabaloos

People shouting and banging saucepans in the street: it's a hullabaloo! Noisy street processions celebrated marriages and all sorts of other events—any excuse at all, really. There were no televisions, and very few people could even read, so they had to entertain themselves.

A Palace Ball

This scene takes place at the height of the Middle Ages, around 1100 A.D. There are 19 items in the picture that did not exist at that time. Can you find them? (Use a magnifying glass if you wish.)

Answers are on page 63.

Game

The building of churches was the great work of the Middle Ages.

Churche

■ Immense Building Sites

The construction of cathedrals was extremely expensive, and took decades, even centuries to complete. ♥ The enormous projects were carried out by stonecutters, sculptors, and all sorts of other craftsmen. The job was supervised by the architect, or master builder.

♥*Work began on the famous cathedral of Notre Dame in Paris in 1163. It was still not quite done in 1245.*

■ The Romanesque Style

There were two styles of architecture in the Middle Ages. The earlier one, used until the eleventh century, imitated Roman techniques. *Romanesque* churches had rounded ceilings, or vaults, which were partially supported by sturdy pillars. The rest of the roof's weight was held up by thick walls.

The Roman church of Sainte-Foye de Conques.

nd Cathedrals

The Gothic Style

At the end of the eleventh century, builders began using a new technique, the ribbed vault. In this method, the entire weight of the roof was supported on the pillars and *buttresses,* or outside supports. Thus, the walls could be opened up for large, ornate, stained-glass windows, and the vault could be raised more than 115 feet (35 meters) high. This *Gothic* style, developed in and around Paris, spread throughout Europe.

The Gothic cathedral of Notre Dame in Paris.

Images in Stone and Glass

The sculptures, statues, and stained-glass windows of both the Romanesque and the Gothic churches illustrated scenes from the Bible and the Gospels. They were designed to tell the story of Christianity to people who could neither read nor write.

Cathedral Schools

Most people received little education. Schooling was most often conducted at the cathedrals, and was intended for the training of future priests. Wealthy bourgeois families hired tutors to teach their children reading and arithmetic—skills for running a business. By the thirteenth century, universities appeared in cities like Paris, Oxford, and Bologna. There, future priests, lawyers, doctors, and teachers received their training.

The gargoyles on Gothic churches sometimes took the form of fanciful dragons and grimacing demons.

The King and the Lords

As the peasants were bound to their lords, the lords were bound in loyalty to their kings. Above them there was only the Emperor and the Pope.

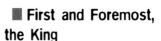

■ First and Foremost, the King

A sacred person, representative of God on Earth, the king ruled alone. He dispensed justice, made war, raised taxes, and spent money at will. But a king had to be on his guard constantly. Royal power was often contested by other monarchs. Even the the nobles, the Church, and at times family members schemed and plotted against the king.

The scepter was a symbol of supreme authority, and the crown represented royal dignity.

The three classes: the religious, the military, and the commoners.

priest   lord   lady   knight   merchant   peasant

◼ Feudal Society

Society was divided into three strictly defined classes. First, there were the men and women of the Church. Their holiness put them above all others. Next, there were the warriors—the knights and nobles. At the bottom were those who worked—peasants, craftsmen, and merchants.

◼ The Great Lords

Some noble families, the dukes, counts, and barons, were extremely wealthy and powerful. In addition to vast estates, they supported many knights as *vassals*. Vassals were obligated to serve their lord in war, in return for which they received land. The power of these lords was sometimes as great as that of their supposed sovereigns, the kings.

◼ Princes of the Church

The vast lands and properties of the Church were ruled by bishops, who were subject to cardinals, who themselves answered to the Pope. These "nobles" of the Church, often themselves of noble blood, had great political influence.

◼ The Great Merchant Families

The rich merchants and bankers were at the top of town society. But, despite their great wealth, they lacked the political power of the nobility.

The Art of Warfare

Owners of the land and leaders in war, the noble lords dominated society.

The Knights

The most feared warriors were the mounted knights. A horse and armor cost a lot of money, and only the noble lords were rich enough to equip themselves. In battle, knights wore coats of steel chain mail and plate armor. Their heads were covered with helmets. Even the horses were *caparisoned* (dressed) in armor. Mounted, the knight fought with a long lance and a broad sword.

A suit of armor often weighed 50 pounds (about 23 kilograms) or more.

Training Started Early

A young nobleman began to train at the age of 8 or so. He did physical exercises and served his lord as a *page*. By the time he was about 13 years old, he became a *squire,* accompanying his lord into battle. Often, by the age of 16, he had proved himself in war, and was *dubbed* a knight. The young man knelt before his lord. In a solemn ceremony, the lord struck him on both shoulders with a sword.

A page became the servant of the king or a noble lord so he could learn how to be a knight.

Jousts and Tournaments

When not at war, knights spent long hours on horseback, hunting wild game They also competed in mounted combats, called *jousts.* Though death and injury sometimes resulted, the knights never tried to kill each other in these *tournaments.* They only sought to prove their bravery.

The Detested Men of War

To help the mounted knights, the kings recruited foot soldiers, armed with spears and knives. Unlike the knights, who sought glory and honor, their job was to kill. Harshly treated and poorly paid, the foot soldiers were held in contempt by the knights.

Squires went to war with their lords.

Military Operations

Great battles were rare. During the Hundred Years War between France and England, armies of only 10,000 to 15,000 troops faced each other. A battle would begin with a cavalry charge from each side, followed by a melee as the sides met to fight under a rain of arrows from the archers.

Masterpiece:

Employed by the Church, the kings, and the lords, artists produced masterpieces of beauty and marvels of invention.

■ Stained Glass Windows

In Gothic churches, beautiful beams of colored light stream in through stained glass windows. To obtain these stunning effects, master glassworkers used rare minerals. Precious lapis lazuli, for example, was crushed into powder to make the gorgeous blue color in the windows of the great cathedral at Chartres.

of the Middle Ages

Illuminated Manuscripts

The printing press had not yet been invented in the Middle Ages. Books were copied by hand, mostly by monks. The monks decorated their manuscripts with pictures, called *illuminations*. Some illuminated manuscripts are masterpieces of miniature painting.

The Introduction of Landscapes in Painting

Because the Church commissioned most art work, almost all paintings were of religious subjects. Jesus, the Virgin, and the lives of the saints were all popular. Figures, drawn in a majestic style, were flat and stiff, with glittering gold backgrounds. In the thirteenth century, Italian artists began to paint more realistically and became interested in details of the landscape. Nobles and the rich merchants had their portraits painted.

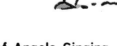

The Sound of Angels Singing

In the Middle Ages music was sacred. Through the perfection of their singing, monks tried to imitate the choir of angels that surrounded God. Choirs were unaccompanied, and everybody sang the same tune, which became known as *plainsong*. Music began to be written down in the eleventh century. About the same time, composers started to write melodies with parts for several voices.

■ **The shoulder collar allowed a draft animal to pull loads six times as heavy as before.**

False. Twice as heavy.

■ **The largest city in the Middle Ages was Rome.**

False. Paris.

■ **Fallow was the name for a tax on bread.**

False. Fallow means leaving ground uncultivated for a year.

■ **The big market towns sponsored regular trade fairs.**

True.

False?

There were often fields and
meadows within towns
in the Middle Ages.

True.

In the Middle Ages
women did not work.

False.

When a young noble became a
knight, his lord
gave him a sharp
blow of the hand
to the nape of
the neck.

False. He struck him on the shoulders with the flat of a sword.

The Gothic
style began in
and around
Paris.

True.

■ **Before the thirteenth century, windows were sealed with oiled paper.**

False. Paper was unknown in Europe until the thirteenth century.

■ **A knight's armor often weighed about 50 pounds (23 kilograms) or more.**

True.

■ **Kings were elected by the People's Assembly.**

False. At first they were elected by the great noble families. Afterward, the title of king was passed from father to son.

■ **Checks date back to the Middle Ages.**

True.

˥alse?

■ In order to cross a bridge or enter a town, you had to pay.

True. This tax was called a toll.

■ In the Middle Ages, potatoes were cultivated everywhere except in England.

False. The potato, which is American, was unknown in Europe in the Middle Ages.

■ In trials, suspects were always tortured.

True. This was what was called questioning.

■ Anyone who was convicted of being a witch was burnt alive.

True.

Index

Animal, 14, 21 38
Architecture
  Gothic, 51
  Romanesque, 50
Armor, 54, 55
Artisan, 28, 29

Bankers, 22, 53
Battle, 38, 55
Beggars, 28, 35, 36
Bishop, 53
Bourgeois, 23, 29, 51, 53
Buttress, 51

Calendar, 15
Cardinal, 54
Carnival, 47
Castle, 12, 16, 17, 27, 41
Cathedral, 38, 47, 51, 56
Charlemagne, 16, 39
Church, 18, 19, 22, 29, 35,
  39, 41, 43, 47, 50, 52,
  53, 56
Cloth, 28, 44
Clothes, 44, 45
Courtly love, 41
Crenellation, 17
Crusades, 31, 37

Drapers, 29
Dubbing, 55

Emperor, 16
Epidemic, 34, 35

Fallow, 15
Famine, 23, 34

Feast, 16, 30, 31, 47
  of the Virgin, 47
Feudalism, 53
Flanders, 23, 29
Flea, 35, 42
Forest, 13, 15, 20, 21
Furniture, 14, 22
Fur, 29, 45

Hat, 44
Helmet, 54
Hermit, 21
Horse, 12, 16, 26, 54, 55
Hullaballoo, 47
Hunting, 16, 21, 55
Hygiene, 34, 42, 43

Illumination, 57
Industry, 28, 29
Isabella of Spain, 41, 43

Jew, 37
Joan of Arc, 41
Joust, 55

King, 37, 38, 52, 53, 55
  King Arthur, 41
Keep, 16
Knight, 41, 45, 54, 55

Lance, 54
Leper, 36
Lice, 42
Loop, 17
Lord, 15, 16, 20, 21, 23, 30,
  41, 52, 53, 54, 55

Manuscript, 19, 57
Master, 28, 29, 50, 53
Medicine, 13, 35
Minstrel, 16
Monastery, 19, 27, 39
Monk, 19, 44, 56, 57

Music, 57
Muslim, 37, 43

Noble, 17, 22, 27, 29, 52, 53,
  54, 55
Nun, 44

Page, 54
Paper, 28
Peasant, 14, 15, 16, 20, 21,
  22, 27, 28, 40, 41, 52
Pilgrim, 26, 27, 39
Plague, 14, 34, 35, 37

Rampart, 22
Religion, 18, 19

School, 51
Serf, 16, 21
Slave, 15
Spices, 31
Squire, 54
Stained glass, 51
Strangers, 21, 36
Sword, 54, 55

Thatch, 14
Tournament, 55
Town, 22, 23, 28, 29, 37, 44

Vassal, 53
Virgin Mary, 39, 41, 46

War, 13, 15, 19, 23, 38, 39,
  41, 44, 52, 53, 54
  Hundred Years War, 41, 55
Wheat, 14
Women, 27, 36, 40, 41, 43,
  45
Worker, 28, 29

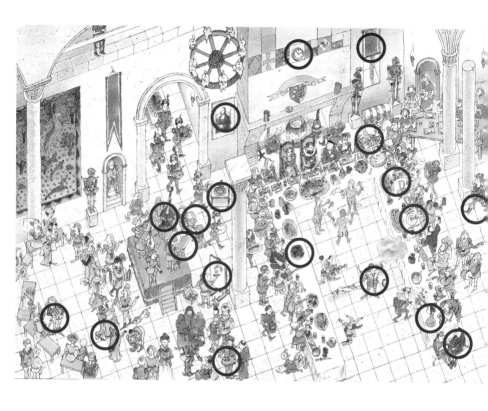

Answers to the puzzle on pages 48–49.

1. a clock (France, sixteenth century), 2. the Mona Lisa (painted by Leonardo de Vinci in 1503), 3. a roller blind (twentieth century), 4. a bass fiddle, 5. a page of a printed book (Germany, 1485), 6. a pencil (invented in 1795), 7. a wheeled cart (late nineteenth century), 8. a fork (sixteenth century), 9. a bottle sealed with a cork (after 1500), 10. china plates, 11. a saltcellar (the saltcellar that was used at this time was simply a little bowl made of wood), 12. tomatoes (called "love apples," and brought from the Americas in 1596, they were initially thought to be poisonous), 13. a stethoscope (nineteenth century), 14. a pocket watch (after 1675), 15. striped clothes (in the Middle Ages, people believed that the Devil could slip in between the stripes and attack you), 16. a zipper (1851), 17. spike heels, 18. boots, 19. a tie.

© 1997 by Editions Nathan, Paris, France.
The title of the French edition is *La vie au Moyen Âge*.
Published by Les Editions Nathan, Paris.

English translation © Copyright 1998 by Nathan LaRousse PLC

Barron's edition adapted by Robert Reis.

All inquiries should be addressed to:
Barron's Educational Series, Inc.
250 Wireless Boulevard
Hauppauge, New York 11788

Library of Congress Catalog Card No. 97-77435
International Standard Book No. 0-7641-5094-4

Printed in Italy
9 8 7 6 5 4 3 2 1

940.1
Bar

Titles in the Megascope series:

Amazing Nature

Searching for Human Origins

Understanding the Human Body

Life in the Middle Ages

Mysteries, True and False

The Pharaohs of Ancient Egypt

Barron's Educational Series, Inc.
250 Wireless Blvd., Hauppauge, NY 11788